HOW BIG IS BIG?

JⱢ

For my children
-S.S.
To Mom and Cookie
-F.4.

Library of Congress Cataloging-in-Publication Data

Strauss, Stephen, 1943-
        How big is big? / by Stephen Strauss; illustrated by the Fernandes Four.
        p.   cm.
Summary: Poetry and facts offer a look at the relativity of measurement terms, such as big and small, fast and slow, deep and high.
        ISBN 0-7613-1664-7 (lib. bdg.)
        1. Size perception—Juvenile literature.   2. Size judgment—Juvenile literature.
[1. Measurement.]   I. Fernandes Four.
II. Title.
BF299.S5S75   1999
153.7'52—dc21   99-14774 CIP

Published in the United States by
The Millbrook Press, Inc.
2 Old New Milford Road
Brookfield, Connecticut 06804
Visit us at our Web site – http://www.millbrookpress.com

Simultaneously published in Canada 1999 by Key Porter Books

Printed in Italy

Cover design by Kathryn Moore

5 4 3 2 1

HOW BIG IS

BIG?

STEPHEN STRAUSS • THE FERNANDES 4

The Millbrook Press   **Brookfield, Connecticut**

If you could take all the water from all the earth's oceans, multiply it by 16, and then make all that water into a ball, that ball would be as big as the moon.

HOW BIG IS BIG?

How big is big?
A super fat pig?
A giant tomato?
A skyscraper potato?
No, bigness is something no one can consume,
Like how many oceans
Fit into the moon.

A dust particle is so small that if you put ten of them on top of one another, they would still be about as thin as a dime.

HOW SMALL IS SMALL?

How small is small?
Something minus-feet tall?
The point of a pencil?
The line on a stencil?
No, smallness is something that's quite hard to see,
Like the fluff in the air
And the dust on your chair.

HOW SLOW IS SLOW?

How slow is slow?
As we all know,
A snail in a hurry
Will never scurry,
But glide at *the* pace
Of a drop of molasses
That drips off your face.

HOW FAST IS FAST?

How fast is fast?
I'm glad *that* you asked.
To walk on water,
You oughta oughta
Use all o' your might,
And double *the* speed
Of a motorbike.

The fastest snail can slither at 27.5 feet (8.4 meters) an hour.

The fastest motorcycle speed is 318 mph (512 km/hr); the speed required to "walk" on water is 671 mph (1080 km/hr).

HOW HIGH IS HIGH?

How high is high?
Well, how high is *the* sky?
I'll say *it* out loud:
It's higher *than* a cloud,
It's where *the* air plays peek-a-boo,
Changing nighttime's black
To daytime's blue.

Between 125 to 185 miles (about 200 and 300 km) up in the sky, the blue sky color ends and becomes black.

HOW DEEP IS DEEP?

How deep is deep?
No, I don't mean deep sleep,
And I don't mean a well,
or a deep prison cell;
But rather imagine *the* fishies' commotion
If a kid ever walked
On *the* bottom of the ocean.

People have descended 35,814 feet (10,915 meters) into the ocean. The deepest spot in the Pacific Ocean is 36,201 feet (11,034 meters) deep.

HOW LIGHT IS LIGHT?

How light is light?
Well, there's light as a kite...
And do you know whether
That's ten times a feather?
But, oh—I think there's been some mistake!
For both weigh much more
Than a single snowflake.

A chicken feather weighs roughly .0007 ounces (.02 grams), and a snowflake only .00000035 ounces (.000001 grams).

HOW HEAVY IS HEAVY?

How heavy is heavy?
Asked a boy named Levy,
Who decided to buy a dinosaur,
But couldn't carry it out of the store.
So he left instead with a lovely toy lion,
Whose weight, while great,
He could lift without try'n.

The largest dinosaur weighed between 110,000 and 175,000 pounds (50,000 and 80,000 kilograms) while the largest lion weighed in at only 690 lbs (373 kg).

The Pacific Ocean is 12,300 miles (19,800 kilometers) wide and stretches between Indonesia and the coast of Colombia in South America.

HOW WIDE IS WIDE?

How wide is wide?
Well, *there's* wide as outside,
And *there's* wide as a smile,
And *there's* wide as *the* Nile,
But wider by far—sort of wideness terrific—
Is *the* width of *that* ocean
They call *the* Pacific.

HOW STRETCHY IS STRETCHY?

How stretchy is stretchy?
It may seem far-fetchy,
But spiders, quite scary,
And sometimes quite hairy,
Make stuff so fantastic,
It's *totally, totally,*
TOTALLY, elastic.

A spider's silk can stretch up to 10 times its original length without breaking. A web made by an American spider has been known to trap a small mouse.

HOW OLD IS OLD?

How old is old?
I have been told
That turtles live long
And trees linger on,
But if true oldness you want to convey,
Then try wishing an amoeba
A happy birthday.

The rhinoceros beetle, which weighs one-tenth of an ounce (only 2.8 grams), can lift 100 times its own weight and walk for a half hour carrying 30 times its own weight! This is like an average-sized man walking one mile (1.6 kilometers) with a car on his head.

HOW STRONG IS STRONG?

How strong is strong?
Consider King Kong,
The movie gorilla,
Whose death was a thrilla.
But even old Kong was monstrously feeble
When compared
To the mighty rhinoceros beetle.

Turtles can live to be 188 years old, and the oldest tree is 12,000 years old. But the oldest living thing is probably a one-celled creature called an amoeba, which started splitting in half about 3.5 billion years ago and has continued splitting ever since.

HOW LONG IS LONG?

How long is long?
You'll be long gone
Once the sun
Ceases to run,
And the only light
Is endless, endless,
Starry night.

HOW BRIEF IS BRIEF?

How brief is brief?
Well, it's my belief
That when you blink,
Or slyly wink,
The time that passes
Is much, much more
Than lightning flashes.

A blink takes about one third of a second, and a wink only about a second. A lightning flash takes about a thousandth of a second.

It is estimated that the sun will burn itself out in 5 billion years. You will likely live about 75 years.

HOW SHAKY IS SHAKY?

How shaky is shaky?
Something kinda earthquaky?
If a mountain of Pekingese,
Those dogs love to tease,
Were to jump from a ladder,
They'd make
The ground clatter.

If 3.5 billion Pekingese dogs jumped from a ladder that was 6 feet 7 inches high (2 meters), they would create an earthquake measuring about 4.5 on the Richter Scale. That's enough to make anything close by, including cars and trees, start to shake.

HOW FULL IS FULL?

How full is full?
Not a belly full of wool,
Not a mountain of hay,
Not Santa's toy sleigh.
No, fullness is more like that quenching of thirsting
Which comes to a camel
Whose drunk till she's bursting!

A camel can drink up to 30 U.S. gallons (114 liters) in ten minutes and 50 U.S. gallons (189 liters) over several hours.

People have walked across coals heated to 1,546°F (841°C). Do not, repeat, DO NOT try this yourself. You will toast your toes.

HOW HOT IS HOT?

How hot is hot?
How hot you got?
I wouldn't choose
To take off my shoes
And go for a stroll
On a flaming bed
Of burning hot coal.

HOW COLD
IS COLD?

How cold is cold?
You'd be quite bold
To stick out your nose,
Or undress your toes,
In any cruel breeze
Cold enough to make
Thermometers freeze.

A mercury thermometer will freeze at -38°F, (-39°C). Your skin will freeze within a half minute at -58°F (-50°C) with a 12 mph (20 km/hr) wind.

HOW SWEET IS SWEET?

How sweet is sweet?
Now *this* poem's a treat.
Though sugar is dandy,
And it rhymes with candy,
Little can give such a sweetening rush,
As the leaves of a green
South American bush.

The Paraguayan plant *Stevia rubidiana* has leaves that are more than 300 times sweeter than sugar. One teaspoon of *Stevia* is equal to about 6 cups of sugar!

HOW MANY IS MANY?

How many is many?
Two dimes or ten pennies?
All grapes in a bunch?
Forty crackers for lunch?
No, many is something beyond stacks and stacks,
It's how much the earth weighs
In piles of Big Macs.

If you were to put the earth on a scale, you would need about 27,800,000,000,000,000,000,000,000 Big Macs on the opposite side to balance it.

HOW CHEWY IS CHEWY?

How chewy is chewy?
What makes gum so gooey?
Each time you bite,
As hard as you might,
The force is so whopping—
Think karate chop, chop,
And then keep on chopping.

HOW HARD IS HARD?

How hard is hard?
Who keeps the scorecard?
It's not baby powder,
Nor soupy clam chowder;
It's not an eggshell, a penny, or brass,
But a diamond so hard,
It slices through glass.

A diamond is the hardest thing in the world. It is much, much harder (10,000 times harder, in fact) than your teeth.

HOW THIN IS THIN?

How *thin* is *thin*?
Well, *there's thin* as a pin.
Then *there's thin* as a sliver
(Ouch! sharp *things* make me quiver).
But *thinness* is something *to* measure with care;
It's a slice, of a slice,
Of a slice, of a hair.

A slice, of a slice, of a slice of a hair is about .00026 inches (about 6.4 microns) across.

HOW THICK IS THICK?

How *thick* is *thick*?
That question's a *trick!*
Thickness is *thinness*, just *turned on its head*,
And one is *the other*, so don't be misled.
I ask you *to* take *ten* heads full of hair,
Glue one *to* another—
And see *thickness* right there.

If you took hair from ten different heads and glued one on top of the other, you'd end up with a pile about 165 feet (50 meters) thick.

On a sunny day after a snowstorm, it is as bright as if you were in a dark closet surrounded by 16,000 lit candles.

HOW BRIGHT IS BRIGHT?

How bright is bright?
Imagine *the* sight
When *the* snow has snowed,
And *the* sun has glowed,
And a little kid sits
Counting 16,000
Candlesticks.

HOW DARK IS DARK?

How dark is dark?
There's as dark as a park
In *the* middle of *the* night,
With no moon in sight,
And a fog billowing billows.
I guarantee
You won't spy armadillos.

If you looked to the sky at midnight on a moonless, overcast night, in a really dense fog, there probably wouldn't be enough light for your eyes to see anything at all.

HOW LOUD IS LOUD?

How loud is loud?
The screams of a crowd?
The snap of your gum?
The bang of a drum?
No, loud is every hurtful noise
That pains the ears
Of girls and boys.

Sound above 130 decibels is painful. That is 100 times louder than the sound of a horn blast from 20 feet (6 meters) away, and roughly twice as loud as the loudest scream.

HOW QUIET IS QUIET?

How quiet is quiet?
Not a schoolyard riot,
Not a loud snore,
And not a dance floor.
No, quiet is something you almost can't hear,
Like the sound that your hair
Keeps away from your ear.

The amount of sound that your hair growing over your ears would block you from hearing is 300 times softer than a whisper.